Drums

Written by Sarah Loader

drum skin

drum rim

drumsticks

Drums are fun.
There are all sorts of drums.

Drums can be hit with a stick,
brush or hands.

Stamp to bang
the big drum.

Drum kits have lots of drums.
There are big drums, toms-toms
and kick drums.

Rock bands have drum kits.

Hand drums do not need sticks.
Hit a hand drum to bang or boom.

Tap fingers on a hand drum to rap and tap.

There are all sorts of hand drums.

Tabla drums are hand drums.
One drum is big and one is little.

Goblet drums are hand drums that fit under the arm.

You can bang a goblet drum
on the rim or on the drum skin.

Marching bands can march and bang the drums.

They bang the drums with drumsticks.

You can hit a drum with a spoon or a brush.

Lots of things can be drums. A pan, a tin or a cup can be a drum.

Pan lids can crash!

It is fun to hit the drums.
Smash! Bang!